Ida Bohatta

The Little Advent Book

English Version by John Theobald

WJ FANTASY

The Angel Choir

Angels have lit their candles in the sky,
And one is peeping in the window now
To see if ours are lit for Him on high,
While other angels flit from bough to bough.
Our light must shine steady and pure and far
To tell the world we're ready for His star.

Making the Manger

We let the little angel in
To help us build the manger.
No room for Jesus in the inn,
So we'll invite the little stranger,
And when He comes our bird will sing.
Shut tight the stable door
To keep the Child from leaving
That heaven's mother bore.

A Heart of Love

At Christmas, angels must bestow
Their presents, bake their cake,
And carry greetings through the snow
Of love, for Jesus' sake.
Yet still they come on Christmas Eve
To bake a golden brown
Heart cookie just for you and leave
It lying to be found.

Borrowing the Crib

"Little donkey, little donkey,
Please lend us your crib.
We'll give it back and oh! we thank'ee!
It's for the Jesus babe."
The gentle beast could never say
A word before to save
His life, but now he brays, "Oh yea!
Take it with all my love!"

Surprise Visits

An angel will protect the Child,
The deer and rabbits keep
Soft watch to make His dreaming mild
As trees at night asleep.
They've brought some straw to make a bed
For one that they revere,
And I have brought some too, to feed
The rabbits and the deer.

Busy Hands

Why is the room lit up so late?
Why does she sew at such a rate?
Why puppy watching in that fashion?
Why little brother filling a cushion?
Why is all this hurry and fuss?
Why, oh why? Well, can't you guess?
If they're not ready, they'll be much sorrow.
It's Christmas tomorrow, tomorrow, tomorrow!

Christmas Greetings

Every city has its fling,
Each gate and path and tinkling bell.
The Christmas spirit knocks and rings
With gifts, more gifts, for arms to fill.
But there's a cottage with no need
For all these presents to be given
Because the children have no greed,
And simply Christmas Day is heaven.

Praying Together

I think the angels are adorning
The baby's room with colors bright.
Cattle are garlanded this morning,
A halo rings the babe with light.
There is a hush of rapture playing,
As if the very walls were praying.
So you
Have a small prayer ready too.